Good Works

Tapping the Practical Power
of Your Core Values

Good Works
Tapping the Practical Power of Your Core Values

STEPHEN SWECKER

RIDERGREEN
BOOK PUBLISHERS

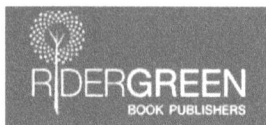

Cover design © 2016 by Rider Green via Canva.com

Library of Congress Control Number: 2013909976

ISBN: 978-0-9819921-9-8 (Paperback)

Also available in digital format:
ISBN: 978-0-9819921-8-1 (ePub version)
ISBN: 978-0-9819921-7-4 (Kindle version)

First printing, June 2013
Second printing, March 2014.
Third Printing, June 2016.

Rider Green Book Publishers
North Berwick, Maine

To my students and Kathy
(not necessarily in that order), whose
good work inspires mine.

≈

"One of the most significant facts
about us may finally be that we
all begin with the natural equipment
to live a thousand kinds of life but
end in the end having lived only one."

Clifford Geertz, **The Interpretation of Cultures**

≈

≈

"Your time is limited, so don't waste
it living someone else's life."

Steve Jobs, **2005 Stanford commencement address**

≈

TABLE OF CONTENTS

INTRODUCTION

"You don't know that old riddle? There's a jungle with a village of truth tellers and a village of liars, and an anthropologist is looking for the truth-telling village. He comes to a fork in the jungle path, and there's a native standing there. What question does he ask?"

Biddy bowed her head for a moment and then looked up, pleased.

"Which way to your village?"...

"Biddy," he said with reluctance, "I have to tell you something."

She snapped the kit closed. "I don't want to hear it," she said firmly. "Wait until after the wedding. Or never. Tell me never, Winn. I don't want to move to the village of the truth tellers. ... Like I said, I'm a realist."

– Seating Arrangements, *by Maggie Shipstead*

Books, articles and sermons proclaiming the practical benefits of values-based behavior, in business as well as our personal lives, are not in short supply in this or any age. Nevertheless, it seems to arrive as a fresh insight whenever a qualified someone comes along and emphatically states that the world works better when our actions spring from our moral selves.

Not surprisingly, a number of such voices arise from the prolific world of religious publishing, such as Pastor Rick Warren's crossover bestseller, *The Purpose Driven Life* (2002). In previous eras, highly regarded works by giants of the genre such as John Gardner (*Excellence*, 1961), Robert Greenleaf (*Servant Leadership*, 1977), Stephen Covey (*The Seven Habits of Highly Effective People*, 1989), and James Autry (*Love and Profit*, 1992) have all made similar points from both functional and values-based perspectives: human beings and their institutions thrive when ethically-grounded priorities direct their behavior.

It depends on whom you ask, of course, whether all of the encouraging words written by these and countless others, past and present, have actually improved the ethical climate. No doubt there's a discernible uptick these days of interest in, if not an actual commitment to, corporate codes of ethics and to ethics training in organizations and companies of all sizes. "Compliance" is a corporate buzzword only slightly less pervasive than "bottom line." Even Internet behemoth's Google's high-minded motto — "Don't be evil." — indicates an awareness of the moral dimension of corporate behavior and the shrewdness of positioning oneself or organization, rightly or not, on the side the good guys.

On the other hand, surveys and research by the Pew Research Center, among others, find that respect for traditional values is declining on many if not all fronts. The decline has been fueled, at least in part, by widespread disillusionment during recent decades with public policies, especially the flawed rationale for the 2003 Iraq war, based on misinformation, deception and questionable intelligence gained through torture.

The picture, in other words, is mixed: There's clearly an interest in knowing where and how the "village of truth tellers" can be found. An active interest in values and morality is not dead. In the name of "realism," though, many of us, like Biddy, are not sure we want to move to the "village of truthtellers." Who wants to risk being infected with naïvtee or, worse, impotence? Afterall, the bad guys, not the truthtellers, appear to be winning. Once again, it seems, we need to be convinced that embracing the truth, whatever is good and right, really "works," i.e., gets results and fulfills our need for meaning.

The dilemma for many Americans is both historical and theological. Recall the quip about our Puritan and Quaker ancestors: "They came to America to do good, and they ended up doing well." It happens to be true. The core values implanted in our New England forebears by their European Christian morality–particularly thrift, honesty and hard work–were a perfect fit for the New World's budding capitalism and its entrepreneurial system of free enterprise.

Sure enough, the virtues of many old-line New England families made them rich (some of their progeny still live just down the road from me here in Maine!). Naturally, as grateful Christians, they attributed their good fortune to their religion, correctly practiced. Their moral conduct, as approved by God, had rewarded them with prosperity and abundance. Success, therefore, was a sign of divine blessing. (Max Weber described all of this in his classic study, *The Protestant Ethic and the Spirit of Capitalism.*)

Ever since (and probably long before), the idea that "doing well by doing good" is a form of divine reward has muddled our understanding of morality and religion. By viewing the fruits of their labor in terms of reward and blessing, our Puritan ancestors paradoxically opened the door for a punitive and judgmental view of those who, unlike themselves, did not prosper and succeed. The formula–success is "reward" (or blessing), failure is "punishment" (or curse)–skewed the causal connection between ethics and outcomes in favor of religion. Morality in this view was simply God's bookkeeping system, His way of keeping score in preparation for the Final Judgment.

We shouldn't be surprised, therefore, that growing doubts about the nature and place of ethics–its "realism," so to speak– have coincided over the decades since the Puritan era with growing doubts about religion and the nature of God– indeed, about the existence of God in the first place!

With that bit of background, we can appreciate the significance of recovering a core insight from our civilization's wisdom tradition prior to its Puritan version. According to more ancient tradition, "doing well by doing good" is *not* a divine reward for being virtuous. Rather, it is the *result* of mastering a vital skill set: sound ethical judgment and conduct. Once we understand the deep tradition's functional (as opposed to theological) linkage of virtue and success, we can regard the core value akin to how the ancients did: as the *built-in operating instructions for the good life of authentic happiness and meaning.*

Recovering that insight, we thus are *liberated from* "morals" as a breeder of *hubris* and an instrument of judgment (divine and human) and *liberated to* embrace life lived in harmony with our core values (i.e., ethics) as an attainable life-skill essential to authentic success.

Hence, in my consulting and coaching practice, I encourage individuals and organizations to "get their values straight" and benefit from strategies for success grounded in their core values. This is not, I remind them, primarily a religious or even a psychological matter (although one can employ either if doing so serves the purpose). Rather, the process of getting our values straight is one of self discovery and practical application, having virtually nothing to do with moralistic notions of getting what we "deserve." In reality, I suspect none of gets what we really deserve– or so we can hope!

This little book does not pretend to be in the same league as its distinguised predecessors in the eternal conversation about values and their relevance to how we live. Nor does it seek to be a rallying cry or prophetic voice for a particular ethical agenda, useful as such can be for illuminating our plight; that's another book for another day. Rather, it is offered in the hope of contributing to the construction of what Rushworth Kidder calls "cultures of integrity" and an effort to reverse, or at least mitigate, an incipient culture of "drowsy" ethics that threatens to doom us.

Merely claiming that task as our goal is somewhat

presumptuous, I suppose. But, it is a deeply felt and invitational turn toward the "village of truth tellers." As such, it accepts the ensuing responsibility to reclaim an urgent piece of ancient wisdom. For if, in fact, ethics is the key to unlocking the operating instructions for being human, there can be no more important job than making that key available to others.

— STEPHEN SWECKER
North Berwick, Maine

≈

"He is happy who lives in accordance
with complete virtue and is sufficiently
equipped with external goods,
not for some chance period
but throughout a complete life."

Aristotle, **The Nicomachean Ethics**

≈

CHAPTER I

Whatever Happened to *Homo sapiens*?

It jumped out at me near the end of a lengthy television interview conducted by NBC's Ted Koppel. He was talking with U. S. Army General Martin E. Dempsey, Chairman of the Joint Chiefs of Staff. To that point, the interview had been something less than riveting, much the usual fare one would expect from a high-level bureaucrat. But, as the conversation was winding down, Mr. Koppel abruptly changed his focus from our nation's infrastructure and its perils to the then-recent resignation, for reasons of adultery, of David Petraeus as director of the C.I.A.

Mr. Koppel acknowledged that very real threats to national security made the "press frenzy" over the personal Petraeus incident seem rather trivial. Even so, he posed the following question to Gen. Dempsey:

"What is it that any commander would not have known beforehand or any man or woman serving under you would not have known beforehand that you've learned from [the Petraeus] situation?"

Gen. Dempsey's response was as surprising as the question:

"We [i.e., his staff] had what I thought was a very healthy conversation about competence and character. And I think potentially over the last ten years, when you're at war, you tend to value competence above all else, naturally. The nation's wellbeing is hanging in the balance. So the first lesson would be — not that we've neglected the character side of this equation, but we're probably at a point where we should re-emphasize it — you can't have a man of incredible or a woman of incredible character who can't deliver on the battlefield because at the end of the day, that's what we're here for. But character counts, and it

counts mightily."

The published interview ended on those words:
"...it counts mightily." I was sorry that the general
didn't have an opportunity on national television to
engage at that point in a "teachable moment." His
emphatic linking of competence and character, and his
emphasis on keeping the two in a working
relationship, was a valuable insight; it was all the more
significant coming as it did from one of the world's
most powerful military leaders. It would have been
instructive to hear from him exactly how and why he
believes that character "counts, mightily."

How, for example, would Gen. Dempsey have
applied that lesson beyond the spectacular moral
failure of David Petraeus to wider issues of the
competence-character equation, not only in the
military but to success in any arena? For, one could
surmise, if the two are as closely linked in an
enterprise as results-oriented as the military, how
instructive must that linkage be for attaining success in
other arenas? The general introduced the concept from
"out of the blue," as it were. So we can infer that it

reflects a deeply held conviction about life itself, and not merely life as a professional soldier.

He's not alone in that belief, of course. But, it's fair to say that, in our success-obsessed culture, which spawns endless books and programs promising sure-fire paths to fame and riches, the link between competence and character — i.e., the moral life and concern for the good, right and true — has been lost on many of us. Indeed, astute observers such as Rushworth Kidder, former columnist for the Christian Science Monitor and founder of a global ethics think tank, have pointed out as much. According to Kidder, we are in the midst of an "ethics recession," that is, a dearth of moral character marked by "selfishness, deception and greed" in both our personal and corporate lives.

Even superficial attention to the news of the day verifies Kidder's assertion. Whether on a personal moral level (gun violence, violence against women, etc.), a corporate level (bank fraud, hazardous environmental practices, etc.), or a societal level (casual disregard of global warming, etc.), an alarming disconnect between core values and our collective behavior is evident. It's not that we don't recognize or care about moral character and ethical issues per se. We absolutely do care, as outrage appears to be growing toward fraud and deception in public life. But, beyond preaching to ourselves about it, it's rare that we *do* anything about it. In this case, "it" is the power failure that results from a) not putting our core values into practice and b) not recognizing that values themselves are essential components of competence, i.e. the ability to get things done.

For example, by comparison, we don't stop caring about money during an economic recession. But, unlike our response when money or employment is in short supply (we strive to get more!), in an ethics recession our response is less certain (how does one *get* more ethics?). Moreover, the vital, life-shaping energy of our core values seems less apparent than the obviously practical benefits of having a job and money. Indeed, it's our argument here that recovering the essential connection between character and competence is at least as crucial for real-world success as the mastery of any other practical skill. Indeed, we believe it *is* possible to "get" more ethics by creating a mindset and a social environment that encourages ethical behavior and the application of core values.

Our ancestors certainly believed this is possible. Ethics in the Western tradition has been regarded as the perennial pathway to meaning, growth and happiness. Its roots can be found in the lives and teachings of the ancient Greek philosophers such as Socrates, Plato and Aristotle. They grappled with the most basic questions and sought what it means to be fully alive human beings. They were our first teachers in the art of living the Good Life, i.e., life that is fulfilling, productive and meaningful. The questions they asked and the principles they discovered remain profoundly relevant to contemporary life, as do the teachings of similarly great teachers through the ages.

This ages-old wisdom is, in fact, one of the generators of advanced human civilization. The reason is not hard to understand: The Good Life, grounded in virtue, is a life that "works." It's a life that acquires the benefits, material and spiritual, that make life worth living in the first place.

So basic is the practical importance of ethical wisdom for humanity that the scientific name for the human species is *Homo sapiens:* Latin *homo* (man) + *sapiens* (wise)*.* The implication is clear: lacking wisdom, we would not be human. It is the attribute of wisdom, understood here as the integration and practice of core values in the business of living, that is essential to being and becoming fully human. As our Greek ancestors, the first modern humans, understood, it does not get more practical than that!

The crisis of our time, however, is that we may be moving from a species that finds its identity shaped less by wisdom and more by attributes other than traditional core values. Or, to state it differently, over time it seems likely that our core values themselves are being challenged and revised, resulting in a competing and seductive alternative "wisdom" that may be re-shaping our self-understanding as a species. In short, *Homo sapiens*, "wise human," may be giving way to *Homo economicus, or* "economic human."

This is not the place to trace this seeming evolution,

but its outline and broad implications are clear enough. Critics of capitalism long have foreseen the threat inherent in the growing concentration of wealth in the hands of a few. The few, in turn, increasingly will control public life and, by extension, the lives of individuals dependent upon its infrastructure. Those who control the means of production (the wealthy few) will require those who do not (the rest of us) to conform to the economic necessity of endless consumption. Our task as *Homo economicus*, in other words, will be to spend and consume, consume and spend — insatiable gerbils wielding our credit cards 24/7 inside the squirrel cages we call "shopping malls." Lost in that dreary scenario will be the life-giving, life-affirming values, especially autonomy and freedom that have been the foundation stones of "wise human" existence across the millennia.

Viewed against this background, ethics — the art of living in alignment with our core values — is on hard times, threatening to become harder. No matter where one casts a spotlight these days — on personal behavior, corporate conduct or government action —

what one inevitably sees varies only with context: life, or lives, swallowed by the quicksand of ethical vacuity and moral hollowness. It no longer requires a preacher or a professional moralist to bring this pervasive aspect of contemporary life to our attention.

So, whatever happened to *Homo sapiens*? The good news is that he/she is not extinct. It's our premise that there's still time to recover the connection with our core values and to experience the power they confer to live fully human lives — lives, that is, that are *sapient* (wise) — and, by doing so, preserve the future of human life itself.

In short, reconnecting character and competence is not only possible but also one of the most urgent challenges of our time. Sometimes, though, it takes a dramatic failure, public or personal, to underscore the vital connection between the two. Such can be an unintended benefit of an ethics recession and a dramatic fall from grace of a respected public figure. They expose the gap between our ideals and our actual condition. At such moments, we have not-to-be-missed opportunities to consider and reclaim the benefits of life pursued in harmony with our core values.

That said, you might well ask, "So, exactly what *is* the connection between character and competence that's exposed when one or the other is revealed to be flawed? Why did General Dempsey link the two in the first place?"

An answer starts with perceptions, specifically perceptions of "mastery." Both character and competence refer to behaviors that are measured by the mastery of critical skill sets. Character links the mastery of moral skills to relationships. Competence links the mastery of technical skills to vocational performance. Perceptions of failed or flawed mastery in either realm, relational or vocational, bring into question the mastery of skills deemed essential for human survival. These include the ability to support trustworthy, stable relationships and the ability to sustain reliable levels of vocational performance (particularly when applied to self-regulated professional conduct).

This perceived connection is primal, perhaps

instinctual, because the linkages bear upon human survival. When perceptions of relational or vocational mastery waver, threads in the social fabric are weakened, particularly the thread of trust. Thus, character and competence supply critical parts of the social glue that holds community together — the military certainly, as General Dempsey understands, but also the wider civil community.

Hence, Dag Hammarskjöld's famous dictum about the peril of indifference to the connection between principles and performance:

"You cannot play with the animal in you without becoming wholly animal, play with falsehood without forfeiting your right to truth, play with cruelty without losing your sensitivity of mind. He who wants to keep his garden tidy does not reserve a plot for weeds."

— Dag Hammarskjöld, *Markings* (1964)

In a sense, what follows is a reflection on keeping our gardens "tidy." It is equally applicable to our personal lives and our life together in community, with an emphasis on the conviction that "character counts, mightily" in both realms. It proceeds by clarifying how we understand our moral selves and stressing close contact with our core values as the operating instructions for meaningful and productive living. Its premise, that "good *works*," is simply a re-stating of what our wisest teachers in the art of living have always tried to tell us: moral excellence and practical success can, and do, go hand-in-hand.

Learning this simple lesson can be the difference between finding happiness in the garden of wisdom (the true home of *Homo sapiens*) or winding up mired in a garden of weeds.

CHAPTER II

Discovering Our Ethical Style: The Four Ways

The most jarring transition in my professional life occurred when I went to work for a national publication as an editorial writer working closely with the newspaper's highly respected editor. I knew his dubious reputation for being demanding and difficult to work with. You can take my word for it: he lived up to his reputation! Twice during the first year of "working together" (I use the phrase loosely), I handed him my letter of resignation, fully intending to end the misery for both of us. Each time, however, he refused to accept the letter. All I could figure was that he somehow was enjoying the pain we were inflicting on ourselves on a daily basis. Sadism was not my thing, however, and I desperately wanted out.

Fortunately, I failed. As it turned out, I worked closely with him for nine years, all but the first being highly productive. We won numerous awards together for the publication and ended up battling side-by-side for causes we believed in. He died prematurely, and, at his deathbed request, I was one of three people designated to speak at his memorial service. It was one of the great honors of my life.

So, what happened in our relationship that resulted in our being able to work together productively for eight years? It was fairly simple, actually: We finally acknowledged that we both cared deeply about many of the same things: clear thinking, good writing, intellectual honesty — not to mention many (but not all) of the social issues that we had to address as journalists and editorial writers for a national publication. Our basic conflict, we discovered, including the way we applied our values to the many situations and topics we addressed, was rooted primarily in our differing ethical styles and how they often led us down very diverse paths. Recognizing that, we found ways to communicate with each other — through our values — on a deep and mostly effective level. We still had our differences, but learned to work together in a spirit of trust, respect and caring. We had found an ethical path forward, and the results rewarded our efforts.

That experience is the primary reason that one of the first things I introduce to my students and clients is a simple template for identifying their ethical style (I regret that it took my editorial colleague and me a year to finally figure it out!). The template distills the wisdom of previous generations into four distinct ways of approaching our ethical decision-making and actions amid the myriad choices we face each day. They are easy to memorize and provide a useful tool for reflection on the Good Life, i.e., on our efforts to live purposefully and meaningfully, and to attain our highest goals: relational, vocational, financial and otherwise. In other words, by directing us back to our moral and ethical foundations, they orient us to a path, or a Way, to tap into the practical power of our core values and apply them to contemporary issues and problems.

In presenting The Four Ways, I associate each of them with the name of a teacher who can be regarded as the founder or exemplar of that particular Way. They are listed in no particular order except for starting, out of respect, with Aristotle, who is generally regarded as the intellectual and spiritual father of the Western ethical tradition.

The Way of Virtue

Aristotle (384-322 BCE)

For those who practice the Way of Virtue, the highest consideration for their decision-making and general conduct is conformity with excellence. For followers of this Way, it is essential that one's life spring from a deep desire to do one's best (excellence of motivation) and that the resulting behavior does, in fact, display qualities of excellence, or virtue, in its relevant particulars (excellence of performance).

A virtuous banker, for example, will display the

excellence of honesty in all of her dealings. Or, a virtuous athlete will display the excellence of strength in the practice of his sport. In any event, The Way of Virtue is grounded in an understanding that a truly human life, i.e., a good life, exhibits qualities that we associate with "character." In all things, therefore, a follower of the Way of Virtue seeks to answer this question:

"What would a person of excellence (i.e., of good character) do?"

The Way of Consequences

John Stuart Mill (1806-1873)

Those who follow the Way of Consequences focus on results. Accordingly, the quality of our decision-making and actions is best measured by the outcomes they yield. The 19th-century philosopher John Stuart Mill believed, as did Aristotle, that an outcome of "happiness" in both personal and public spheres of life is the proper goal of living. In this view, the Good Life is one whose choices and conduct result in happy outcomes.

An important aspect of this Way is the ability to anticipate the likely consequences of one's behavior. For example, a legislator following this Way would try to foresee the social impact of a proposed law. Thus, one who follows the Way of Consequences regularly engages in a kind of "moral calculus" that assigns cost-benefit value to the likely results of one's actions. The aim is to produce "the greatest happiness for the greatest number," as Mill memorably stated it.

Therefore, a follower of the Way of Consequences seeks to answer this question:

"What choices and/or actions will produce the best results, i.e., the greatest happiness for the most people?"

The Way of Rules

Immanuel Kant (1724-1804)

The guiding principle for one who follows the Way of Rules is alignment of one's choices and actions with universal moral laws — OR (and this is crucial) with behavior that one would desire to become universal moral law, i.e., applicable to everyone for all time.

Doing one's duty, i.e., obeying and upholding the rules of moral conduct as learned from one's culture or tradition, is the essence of the Good Life for followers of this Way.

The appeal of the Way of Rules for its followers is its orderliness, predictability and stability. Moral laws, such as "Do not kill," "Do not lie" and "Do not steal" are — or at least appear to be — permanent. As such, they are anchors amid a sea of constant change and occasional turbulence. And, its advocates would say, if each of us always behaved in ways that we would want all people to behave — as though our actions were writing the rules for the human race! — the world would be a saner, wiser place.

For that reason, the abiding challenge for one who travels the Way of Rules is:

"What rule(s) should I practice and model for others, i.e., what is my duty in the circumstances that are facing me?"

The Way of Compassion

H. Richard Niebuhr (1894-1962)

This Way goes by many similar names: the Way of Love, the Way of Caring or, even, the Way of Responsibility (in a modern interpretation by H. Richard Niebuhr); however understood, it is the way of responding with compassion to all people in all circumstances at all times. For many, particularly those whose sense of morality is rooted in a religious or spiritual tradition, the Way of Compassion is summarized by some version of the Golden Rule: "Do to others as you would have others do to you." For such people, the words of songwriter John Lennon ring true: "Love is all you need." Instead of many rules, there is only one rule for followers of this Way: Always do what love requires.

There is no question that some of history's wisest teachers have proclaimed and lived the Way of Compassion, to the great benefit of humanity. From the Buddha and Jesus to Gandhi and Martin Luther King, Jr., followers of this Way point to the healing impact of love on relationships among friends and adversaries alike. Furthermore, they believe that one who practices love also is healed by the energy that returns to them through their acts of love.

Therefore, the question asked by one who follows the Way of Compassion is:

"What is the most loving (compassionate, caring, responsible) thing to do?"

* * *

Two concluding observations can be noted about the Four Ways:

First, it's likely that most of us feel a basic comfort level with one or, at most, two of the Four Ways, and that we tend to operate primarily from that perspective. Hence, identifying "our" Way, and gaining deeper insight about it, is a practical step toward "knowing thyself." Knowing our Way — both our primary Way and our secondary or back-up Way — helps us to recognize our ethical bias, that is, our default approach to moral judgment and action. Armed with that awareness, we are able to compensate for it at times when we're stumped or when we're seeking to reconcile competing or conflicting viewpoints.

Second, we should emphasize that all Four Ways are principled approaches to the challenge of ethical reasoning and living. No single Way is inherently superior to any other Way. Embracing this knowledge liberates us from being judgmental about Ways that differ from ours. It also offers the possibility that we can expand our individual capacity for living wisely and meaningfully by benefitting from the insights of those with an ethical bias toward Ways that differ from ours. That's why I recommend to my students and clients that they learn a "back-up" Way to approach ethical problem solving beyond their default or natural Way. Such ethical dexterity is a key survival skill in a world of growing diversity and complexity

There are other Ways to pursue ethical matters, of course: the Way of Self-Interest, the Way of Pleasure, the Way of Expedience, and so forth. All are widely practiced and contribute to the moral cacophony and confusion of our time. But, all of the other Ways beyond the traditional Four Ways have a similar fatal flaw: they turn us inward, and ultimately frame our moral or ethical choices in terms of self-interest, i.e., their benefit for me and/or my kind.

In contrast, each of the Four Ways compels us to look outward toward a "bigger than self" vision of life. Therefore, each inclines toward a vision of being human that invites growth, generosity and goodness of spirit for its own sake and not merely what it will do for "me." This quality of "outwardness," as we later will see, is essential to authentic happiness and the quality of experience that we call *meaning*.

Eventually, I would recognize that my combative editorial colleague and I not only survived but thrived over the years because we found meaning in our work together. It was meaning made possible because we learned to identify our shared values despite, and sometimes because of, the differing Ways we realized we were taking in our approaches to life itself. Our ethical empathy, if one can call it that, lent fresh insight into poet Robert Burns' famous line:

"O wad some gift the Giftie gie us, To see oursels, as ithers see us."

Discovering the Four Ways was, for the two of us, the gift that helped us see "oursels" *and* each other.

CHAPTER III

Drilling to the Core: Unlocking the Code

Certain moments stand out in our lives for a reason. To find that reason, strip away the drama, the elements of surprise, pain, joy, shock, or whatever the emotional impact might have been at the time. Eventually, you will find, underneath it all, something at work far deeper than what you felt at the time, and more durable, too. That "something" will be more than the images — visual, auditory, spiritual, etc. — that have stuck with you and that remind you of the original experience. It, in fact, will arise from our human core, the deepest part of us that harbors and generates the values that guide and shape us throughout our lives —provided, that is, we claim them and allow them to empower us.

Such a moment early in my life gave me an opportunity to do just that, i.e., the stripping away or what is referred to below as drilling (a term that I use shamelessly despite some of its anti-environmentalist connotations!). Here's what happened:

I was a student in graduate school at George Washington University studying international relations and preparing, I hoped, for a career in the foreign service of the U.S. Department of State. In one of my seminars was another student, some ten years older than me, who was living a life much like the one I envisioned someday for myself. As a State Department employee, this very bright fellow had just returned from duty as an information officer in South Vietnam where the United States was engaged in an escalating, very controversial war. He was quite eloquent, and frequently regaled us kids (which, in comparison to him, we definitely were) with stories about the war and his observations about the U.S. military presence in South Vietnam.

I particularly remember that he frequently wore bright red socks that protruded from his khaki trousers; they were very visible when he stretched his legs under the seminar table directly across from me. So cool! I really admired the guy and was hoping I could emulate him right down to the red socks … until, that is, he gave a lurid but dispassionate description in class one day about an especially brutal U.S. military operation he had witnessed against the enemy. From his graphic description, certain things about that action were clear: our soldiers slaughtered the inhabitants of a village "believed" to harbor the enemy; the slaughter was reported as a defensive action by his information office; and, although he didn't view the carnage as defensive, he had no problem with reporting it as such to protect the reputations of the soldiers and officers, many of whom he knew personally.

After he finished his dramatic story, I was stunned. It was so unvarnished and so horrific that I nearly threw up in disgust. Then and there, my whole life changed. I knew that I could never be part of what he had just described, and any desire I had to follow his career path vanished in an instant — right down to the socks.

It took weeks of self-searching, including a spur-of-the-moment counseling session with a church pastor that I didn't know, to sort out what had happened. I came to see that I was engaged in a titanic struggle for self-knowledge at that point, because everything I thought I knew and wanted, vocationally at least, had just left the building. But, when insight finally emerged, I realized that the experience in the seminar room had brought me face-to-face with a deep part of myself, best described as an abhorrence of violence and efforts to justify it, even in the name of patriotism. I had, in short, discovered a core value — for me — of non-violence and its companion ethical principle: *Do no harm*. Claiming and releasing that basic moral framework helped profoundly to shape my life in the years that followed, from my professional work to parenthood to individual relationships.

I tell this personal episode to illustrate an important lesson for identifying and connecting with our moral selves: Far from being an exercise in abstraction, drilling into our own stories, particularly the "big moments" or crises that we remember for their impact on our lives, yields empirical evidence of our core values and the power they hold for shaping our existence. What makes core values "core," in other words, is the deep control or authority they provide for guiding our actions and preserving our humanness.

The operative word, as noted above, for discovering empirical evidence of our core values is "drilling." The approach to character formation advocated here, leading to moral growth and the practical benefits of ethical fitness, is based on deep self-knowledge acquired through selective reflection on our experience. The premise is simple but liberating: A key to freedom and empowerment, both individual and organizational, is discovering and applying the *values that surface* during life's inevitable crises.

Both historical evidence and emerging research show that powerful solutions for individuals and organizations can occur, sometimes with astonishing speed, when we finally "get our values straight." When we acquire a clear-eyed view of what our core values are and act to bring ourselves into alignment with them, it's like being yanked abruptly into an awareness of our true selves and hearing our marching orders, as if for the first time.

Thus, to know and claim our core values is to unlock the code to success and wellbeing. It sounds so basic, and it is. For that reason, perhaps, acknowledging the power of our values to direct and empower our lives eludes us because we're looking for something more exotic or esoteric. We want to know the "secrets" that will get us what we want. The secret, however, is this: *There is no secret*! We have known about the power and wisdom of value-driven lives since the Greek philosophers, if not earlier!

In our consumer culture, one of the surest ways to test the validity of such propositions is to find out how, or if, they apply in the market place (yes, we can learn something about *Homo sapiens* by observing *Homo economicus*!). For example, the New York Times (2/13/2013) reports that a number of corporations are finding that what they call "purpose marketing" — defined as projecting a company's core values — is achieving significant bottom-line results. "Purpose marketing is becoming popular on Madison Avenue because of the growing number of shoppers who say that what a company stands for makes a difference in what they do and do not buy," according to the Times. The report continued:

" 'We talk about our values internally, but we've been reticent to leverage them,' Mr. Simon [a Panera Bread Company executive] said. That changed as a result of research that showed that communicating those attributes and actions could be 'more compelling to our customers' than conventional pitches about meal deals or how 'my sandwich is better than the guy across the street's.' "

For example, Panera's daring experiment to help address growing food insecurity in the United States by opening community cafés with no cash registers or prices appears to be working. Donations are requested from those who can afford to pay, but those who can't are able to eat for free. Not only are "free cafés" paying for themselves, but Panera also appears to be reaping spillover goodwill via the growing profitability of its regular stores.

In other words, sell your character, the outward projection of your core values — perhaps even before selling competence (although you certainly do need a quality product!). The reason is no mystery: We are attracted to displays of authentic moral substance, perhaps because such displays elevate our game as humans. Authenticity inspires. It places us in the presence of something we experience, indeed yearn for, as real and genuine. These are qualities that are hard to resist in a world where television producers sell us pre-scripted, tightly controlled pseudo-dramas and call them "reality shows."

We shouldn't be surprised, then, that values-based strategies such as "purpose marketing" work. They promote trust by putting authenticity on public display. Their validity is grounded in the ancient wisdom that "the truth which sets us free" resides within ourselves — or, in the case of Panera Bread Company, within a corporate culture that has made the effort to drill for its core values and learned how to project and give life to them in the marketplace.

Discovery of individual or corporate truth is, in fact, a key to unlocking the door to richer, deeper, more rewarding experience: relationally, vocationally, materially and spiritually. Living in harmony with our core values liberates us to pursue what Robert Hargrove calls our "impossible future," a beckoning vision or shining cause that we otherwise might consider out of reach. Such character-based living is revolutionary and transformative. The lives and teachings of great teachers such as Socrates, Confucius, Jesus and the Buddha testify to this lesson. Theirs was an empirical, deeply practical approach to the Good Life based on self-knowledge of the kind that results from drilling for our core values. Little wonder that character-based living has stood the test of time and is as applicable to contemporary life as it was to the ancient world.

In drilling for our core values, therefore, we find clues in classical ethics about what to expect. We situate these clues in "classical" ethics for the simple reason that they have existed for so long as to be almost clichés when we talk about character, morality

32

and ethics. The guidance that they offer in any specific situation or set of circumstances can seem vague, so minimal are they with regard to specific content. But, used as the drill bits (to extend our engineering analogy) for digging into the Big Moments of our lives and extracting the underlying values, they become highly useful — so useful, in fact, that they can be regarded as the Three Essentials:

Do right. Be true. Seek good.

These three familiar moral dictums are essential, one might say, because they help us get to the bottom of our search (or drilling) for our core values. On closer examination, we recognize that they are, in fact, a summary of all core values.

For example, "Do right" embraces all that we include under the banner of moral or ethical rules, such as the Ten Commandments of Judaism and Christianity or the Five Precepts of Buddhism. The concept of rules also includes the entire arena of positive or civil law, obedience to which is *prima facie* ethical; that, at least, is true to the extent that the laws themselves do not violate ethical principles and serve in practice to make life in community safe, orderly and as fair as possible.

Or, "Be true" captures the range of virtues that starts with the principle of truth telling and extends into all arenas of life in which alignment with the truth is critical to maintaining human community. Values such as trust, honesty, loyalty, commitment, promise-keeping — all values that supply relational glue to our experience — are grounded in one way or another in our willingness to honor truth. Scarcely any community, whether a family, an academic department or an emergency room staff, can function without a basic commitment to truth. Likewise, personal integrity depends upon our capacity for being honest with ourselves as well as with other people.

Finally, "Seek good" foresees the task of living as being to promote all manner of well being, the *shalom* of ancient Israel, the "common good" of Roman Catholic moral theology and the "public interest" of secular humanism. Although it naturally illuminates our relationship to others and our life in society, it also implies a sense of self-referring values that honor selfhood: be well, be healthy, take care of yourself. Understood in both its social and personal dimensions, "Seek good" points to a constellation of core values that seem to be absolutely essential to preserving human life in the face of threats such as global warming and nuclear cataclysm.

The Three Essentials, in other words, are what we might call "super values." By distilling the wide range of possible core values into three summary or super values, they perform the helpful task of orienting us as we sort through our experience and seek the underlying core values that shape and enliven us.

In my own Big Moment mentioned at the beginning of this chapter, it's easy to see how deploying the Three Essentials would have been an immediate help for drilling through the profound disillusionment of my seminar awakening. Each one of the three would have provided a clue to my dis-ease and pointed me to a value, or set of values, that I was aligned with and empowered to express through my subsequent behavior. **Do right:** *I reject brutality.* **Be true:** *I cannot deflect or obscure responsibility for violent* *misconduct, including my own.* **Seek good:** *I must refrain from violence and encourage others to do the same.*

My guess is that Panera Bread Company and other similarly socially responsible companies are using these super values to drill into their cultures and find the core values that form the basis for "purpose marketing" their products. Once these values are discovered, because they were part of the corporate culture all along, it isn't necessary to "bolt on" strategies or slogans that aren't authentic expressions of the organization. Rather, they can base their marketing on who they *really* are, and by doing so experience the many benefits of simply being themselves, including real-time, bottom-line success.

What's true for corporations in this regard also applies to individuals. Apple Computer founder Steve Jobs famously told a Stanford graduating class: "Your time is limited, so don't waste it living someone else's life." In practice, he might have added that there's only one reliable way to do just that: take the time and make the effort to drill for your core values, the values that are the deepest expression of who you are and what you stand for. Once you've done that, you are free and empowered to live the only life worth living: Yours. To start? *Do right. Be true. Seek good.*

CHAPTER IV

Good Works: Getting from Values to Solutions

H ere's a hunch: Examine the lives of extremely
productive people, and you will find in nearly
every case individuals with a clear sense of their core
values and the connection of those values to their
life's work. Their character and their competence will
be seen to be inseparable.

Take the life of the extraordinary German
polymath, Albert Schweitzer. A musician, author,
theologian and medical doctor, Schweitzer lived until
the age of 90 doing what he loved. Among other
things, he wrote a seminal work on ethics in which he

identified what for him was the core value at the heart of all morality: reverence for life. It turns out that he spent much of the last decades of his life in Lambaréné, Gabon as a medical missionary, founding a hospital that exists to this day, giving concrete expression to that single ethical principle. One of his biographers said of the significance of those years: "He never really stopped [living his values]. In fact, there's a lot of contemporary research which shows that if you do a job that engages your ethics, it will give you more satisfaction than prioritizing money or status." Schweitzer himself once said, "The values that are turned into will and action constitute a richness that must not be undervalued."

A more recent observation about the link between values and outcomes makes a similar point. It comes from technology executive Willem Roelandts, writing in the Harvard Business Review (June 12, 2012):

"Early on in my career I wondered what made people put their whole hearts and souls into their work. The stock answer was: 'Pay them more and they will contribute more.' But I have found that is

not the case. What really motivates people is the idea that they are doing something useful and meaningful. Doing something useful and making meaningful contributions imply that you can be a leader, that you can decide on what to work on, and that you can influence your work — and can make a difference."

"Doing something useful and meaningful," of course, invites the question, "In relationship to what?" If the "what" is merely the company's bottom line or corporate growth, our hearts are little stirred. It's clear from the context, though, that Roelandts is referring to something deeper, something capable of drawing people's "hearts and souls" into their work. From the extraordinary lives of people like Albert Schweitzer and his kind, and from the studies by leadership experts such as Stephen Covey (*The Seven Habits of Highly Effective People*) and Jim Collins (*Built to Last: Successful Habits of Visionary Companies*), we know what the "something" is to which Roelandts refers: It is the direct and undeniable link between values and results. Get the former right and the latter follow. Align our work with our core values, and we are not merely *motivated*, as Roelandts says; we are actually *empowered* to do extraordinary things.

In short, experience and observation show that the main title of this essay is absolutely true: good *works*. Similarly, character *builds*. And, values *produce*. State it however you wish, or however cleverly you might, the lesson is the same and equally powerful: The source of authentic success is found in our moral depths. Know and claim — truly claim — your core values, and the rest is merely strategy.

At this point, you might well ask how the relationship between what we call ethical clarity (discovering and claiming our core values) and getting results, in fact, *works*. Following are brief descriptions and some examples summarizing how ethics:

• catalyzes our thinking and makes the outcome more productive;

• illuminates the content of behavior and helps us know what is really going on;

• helps to separate what is truly important from the less important or trivial;

41

- provides a "cooler" way to deal with emotion-charged dynamics; and

- creates an environment for stable future relationships, i.e., promotes trust.

Let's look briefly at each of these functions of ethics.

Catalyzes our thinking and makes the outcome more productive

In his seminal book on ethical decision-making, Rushworth Kidder presents the idea of core values as "moral reagents" or catalysts. When identified and introduced into our thought and conversation, core values can clash and erupt as energizing conflict, heightened creativity, or both. Operating in this way, ethics can be catalytic in nearly any arena, both individual and organizational. The introduction of core values into the conversation, Kidder says, "has an uncanny way of stimulating the process." The situation at hand takes on a conceptual and perceptual "sharpness," and ultimately a behavioral focus, that it otherwise would lack without the stimulus of ethical content and the spirited interplay of core values.

Illuminates the content of our thought and behavior

One of the most important tasks in any situation is to figure out what we're *really* dealing with. The introduction of core values — perhaps starting with the Three Essentials, or super values — throws light on the matter and helps us see what is really at stake, and why we care to begin with. Hypothetical examples (and not, mind you, prescriptions): "What we're really talking about here is *trust*" (say, in a marital conflict). "What we really are fighting about is *fairness*" (say, in a corporate take-over bid). "What we're really trying to protect is *intellectual honesty*" (say, in an academic dispute). In fact, when we're tempted to use "really" as an adverb to describe what's going on, we're probably preparing to introduce what we regard as the core value that's at stake and therefore most important.

Helps separate the important from the trivial

My newspaper colleague, referred to in Chapter II,

liked to point out "rabbit trails" in our editorial drafts. By that, he was identifying places where we had raised an issue that was secondary to our main point, or where we had introduced a line of reasoning that could confuse the reader about the main point. The issue rarely was whether the rabbit trail was interesting or valid. The issue was, is the new idea that it introduced essential to making the point of that particular editorial? If not, it was a rabbit trail, a diversion from the main trail. Having identified our point, or core value, for that particular editorial, we could distinguish the important main idea from other less important ideas. Thus, we avoided taking ourselves and our readers down distracting, time-wasting rabbit trails.

Provides a "cooler" way to deal with emotional dynamics

A student believed he had grounds to challenge the course policy of not allowing make-up quizzes. He expressed emotional distress about the matter to his instructor (me), and with understandable cause: illness and domestic problems out of his control made him miss the quiz. I felt my own frustration rising, however, as he made his tearful case that, in his specific situation, I should be willing to suspend the no-make-up-quiz policy. I believed I couldn't do that and still pretend it was a meaningful policy; after all, *everyone* has a reason for why they are an exception.

Finally, I was able to bail us both out of the emotional brew. I re-cast our impasse as an impersonal case study, much like the ones we frequently discussed in class. So, I asked him, what was the moral issue in "that" impersonal situation? "Fairness," he said, unhesitatingly. To whom? "Fairness to other students." Bingo. The light went on. The emotional bomb was diffused. He dropped his request. Lesson: Finding an ethical perspective on tense situations and identifying core values can help cool passions and clear the way for less emotionally-tinged problem solving.

(*Caution*: Emotions and passions are not "bad" from an ethical standpoint. They can serve as "ethical radar," pointing to moral issues and asking that we pay attention. But, as a warning system, they best stand at the start of ethical reflection as an impetus, not at the end of reflection as a resolution. Example: Is it ethical to get your way by pouting or sobbing? Probably not.)

Creates an environment for stable relationships

In our psychology-saturated culture, discussion and openness about personal feelings are highly prized. A case can be made that it's healthy to "let it all out" and avoid the harmful stress of unexpressed feelings. But, even acknowledging its possible benefits, the expression of feelings itself is an inherently unstable basis for whatever comes next in a relationship or situation. Feelings trigger yet more feelings. You've been there, and so have I (see the previous story).

By contrast, basing communications, when possible, on core values creates an altogether different kind of environment. It's an environment anchored in the reliability of values themselves, which function as a code to ensure that we "remember" our basic commitments as *Homo sapiens*. In other words, when we can interact with each other on the basis of values, we can be reasonably certain that the person we dealt with yesterday will be the same person we deal with tomorrow. Values and how we apply them can change, of course. But, in general, they change not nearly as quickly or disruptively as our feelings and passions.

• • •

In a preliminary way, we now can see how our core values, whether expressed as attributes of character, ethical clarity or moral virtues, supply both direction and energy for seeking practical solutions and achieving real-world goals. In this functional sense, they supply the code for successful living. The code is drawn from the depths of what it means to be human and transcends any particular cultural, religious or political expression: honesty is honesty, whether one is a Hindu, a Brazilian or a Republican. Likewise with fairness, compassion, loyalty and a host of other universally recognized virtues.

Therefore, it isn't necessary to moralize, preach or proselytize to demonstrate that character is an essential accompaniment to competence, or that competence is, in part at least, an extension of character. Both, as stated earlier, point us to the mastery of skills — including the application and practice of core values

— essential to engendering trust and ensuring human survival. Through the practice of The Four Ways and the application of The Three Essentials, we find that we possess the basic tools needed to reflect upon, analyze and direct our thought and behavior toward these practical ends in every aspect of our lives.

CHAPTER V

A System of Values: The Success of Meaning

I was gratified to see a recent article in The Atlantic Magazine (Jan. 9, 2013) that re-introduced the world to the groundbreaking work of the Austrian psychiatrist Victor Frankl. Dr. Frankl's landmark 1946 volume, *Man's Search for Meaning*, was named in the 1990's by the Library of Congress as one of the 20th century's ten most influential books. A Jewish Holocaust survivor, Frankl was a heroic figure, not only for his profound writing and insight into the human condition, but for the moral quality of his personal life. More than once at critical moments, he put himself in mortal danger by risking his own life to protect or care for others. For example, his decision to turn down a chance to immigrate to the United States and remain instead in Austria to be with his aging parents was an all-but-certain death sentence. Indeed, his parents, along with the rest of his family, perished in Nazi concentration camps. Frankl himself survived against all odds, a story he tells with gripping poignancy in *Man's Search for Meaning*.

Relevant to our interests here, the Atlantic Magazine discusses Frankl's work under the heading, "There's More to Life Than Being Happy." It contrasts the contemporary American quest for individual happiness with Frankl's emphasis on *meaning* as the defining attribute of a well-lived life, i.e., a good life. Happiness, researchers have found, is mostly about "feeling" good, while meaning is about "doing" good. The difference in behavior and results is dramatic. Studies find that those who seek happiness as the *raison d'être* of their lives tend to be self-centered, "takers" rather than "givers." By contrast, those who seek meaning and purpose tend to incorporate giving

to, and even sacrificing for, others in their lives —
even at the possible expense of superficial happiness.
Central to the meaning-filled life, researchers have
found, is the ability to endure hardship and suffering
and to display a sense of responsibility to something
greater than the self.

Hence, according to Frankl:

*"Being human always points, and is directed, to
something or someone, other than oneself — be it a
meaning to fulfill or another human being to
encounter. The more one forgets himself — by giving
himself to a cause to serve or another person to love
— the more human he is...[Such a person] knows the
'why' for his existence, and will be able to bear almost
any 'how.'"*

Meaning, therefore, understood as a *system of
values* that empowers and sustains life, emerges as an
indispensable component of the Good Life — indeed,
it's the "defining attribute," as stated above. *To live a
meaningful life is to live in conscious relationship with
core values that command our allegiance, summon our
energies, and call us out of ourselves to a sense of*

responsibility for something greater than ourselves.

Now, with the help of Frankl's concept of meaning, we can recognize the vital connection between our core values and the ancient Greeks' idea of *virtue* as the key attribute of a well-lived life. It goes like this:

Both meaning and virtue, viewed as the "bundling" of our core values into a way of life, *attune* us to that which is good, right and true. They form a moral skill set that a) gives content to and receives guidance from the faculty we call *conscience*, b) provides motivation and energy for deciding and acting as people of *character*, and c) inclines us in all things to seek *excellence (competence)*. Stated as a formula, it looks like this: *Attunement to Core Values > Conscience + Character + Competence = Virtue*. It is, in other words, a formula for what Aristotle called a "complete life" and what Victor Frankl called meaning.

The above is highly condensed and a lot to digest in one gulp. Its formulaic nature may be off-putting to some, at least initially. But, unpacked, it helps us to reflect anew on the close connection between core values and the character/competence dyad. Properly understood, the same core values that shape our character also shape our competence and pursuit of excellence. Through experience, we come to realize that meaning, virtue and character are not merely *good*. They are good for *something*! They actually engender excellence and competence. They get practical results. In the best sense, they *succeed*.

Or, to paraphrase Frankl, a meaningful life not only knows the "why" for one's existence. It also is able to envision and give rise to the "what," namely, success.

At this point you are forgiven if you are thinking that the case being made in this essay for the importance of value-laden ideas such as character and meaning has exaggerated the benefit of virtue at the expense of life's practical side. Character has swallowed competence, you might argue (although we believe the above formula refutes that notion). After all, you could point out — accurately — that countless people of unassailable character do not succeed. A cynical observer might go further and argue "the good die young while evil flourishes as the green bay tree." Whatever one might think of such pessimism, it's undeniable, as General Dempsey has observed, that "incredible character" alone is insufficient to meet the requirements of living a fulfilling life.

In response, we would say that the case being made here is for the restoration of an overdue balance to a two-sided coin, that being the quest for a well-lived or good life, sometimes described as success. Both sides, character and competence, are needed to complete the coin. The divorce of the two serves no advantage, unless one regards expedience as a value. Rather, divorcing the two leads to a shriveled, trivialized vision of success regardless of one's perspective.

For example, success built solely on a foundation of competence is hollow and transient, lacking the spiritual substance and social glue needed to endure. Similarly, success sought solely through virtuous behavior and good intentions founders on the hard rock of naïveté and human fallibility. These are extreme scenarios, of course, but they help to illustrate an underlying convergence: the need to keep character and competence in a dynamic balance in which each draws upon and reinforces the same set of core values.

Competence, in other words, is by no means a minor concern, particularly in the United States; by almost all measures, U.S. society is falling behind the rest of the industrialized world in the STEM disciplines: science, technology, engineering and mathematics. The current problem, however, is that character and the moral basis for success are even more neglected, what with our society's legitimizing wealth as power and winning at all costs. As a result, we are paying a high price for that neglect in the form of a debilitating ethics recession and a cynical search for superficial happiness rather than genuine meaning and purpose. Little wonder that experiencing the Good Life for too many is ephemeral and elusive. Thus, "The Amazing Race" television "reality" show is a metaphor of our time: a frantic, silly chase after wealth and celebrity that is as fleeting as it is trivial.

The good news is that this state of affairs is being recognized, at least in some quarters, and that efforts are being made to remedy it. We have given examples of such efforts in both personal and corporate settings, but have not addressed how more widespread efforts are being, or might be, implemented. Our premise has been that we need to grasp the problem and what's at stake before we are in a position to tackle its solution. There's a time for "Ready" and a time for "Aim" (both of which we've tried to do). What's needed now is "Fire," the igniting of concrete efforts to bring the operating code of core values to the surface of our deliberations and actions, both personal and public.

(For starters, a list of "Eleven Ways to Join (or Start) an Ethics Revolution" is included in the Appendix. The idea is to initiate conversations and generate questions and ideas, not to yield immediate answers and solutions, important as finding such ultimately will be. Ethics is not about quick fixes.)

Although extricating ourselves from the ethical mire in which we find ourselves can't happen overnight, changes in behavior can start anytime. The re-uniting of character and competence through small deeds and modest acts of consciousness-raising is a realistic strategy that is both necessary and doable without special training. By applying the Four Ways, drilling for core values and linking them to the quest for genuine meaning, we can find a path forward for creating cultures of integrity and re-discovering the Way of Wisdom.

Hopeful for now is that Victor Frankl's profound lesson about the need for meaning in our lives is being recognized once again as a matter of survival, both individually and collectively. Central to that recognition is this: *Meaning-filled lives do, in fact, succeed; they are successful by definition.* And we know that such lives are built on an allegiance to an embodied code of core values and an outward-facing sense of responsibility to and for others. It's that simple but, at the same time, it's also that challenging.

An ethics revolution will have begun for real when this awareness is planted in the minds and hearts of a critical mass of the Earth's people. When that moment arrives — and it *must* arrive if there is to be a human future and an Earth to care for — we will experience not only the meaning of authentic success. We also will have reason to celebrate the success of meaning.

APPENDIX

Eleven Ideas for Joining (or Starting) an Ethics Revolution

• Start an "ethics soup kitchen." Idea: Set a time and place for a simple meal and open discussion of everyday ethical issues. The topics can be contributed by the participants or taken from "The Ethicist" column of the New York Times Sunday magazine.

• Circulate (by email, Facebook or Twitter) a list of recommended books on meaning, values-based living, practical ethics, etc. Depending upon your

special interests, consider authors such as Victor
Frankl, Stephen Covey, Jim Collins, Peter Singer,
and others who deal with these themes in a holistic
or 360° perspective.

• Identify the top five core values of your religious
tradition or a tradition that interests you. Connect
those values to your relationship goals. To your
vocational goals. To your financial goals. To your
"impossible future."

• Choose a Core Value of the Month (or week).
Reflect on your experience of it. What Big Moment
or life crisis revealed it to you? Research it. Who
would be its patron saint (if you think in such
terms)? Discuss its importance and role in your life
around the dinner table.

• Start a study group to identify and discuss core
values and their link to behavior, especially
outcomes regarded as successful. Focus on their
practical benefits.

- Identify a problem in your personal life, your family or your organization's life. What are the core values at stake? How might identifying them and discussing them help turn a problem into an opportunity? If acted upon, how could things be different?

- Interview three people whom you regard as successful (relationally, financially, emotionally, etc.). How do they view their particular success? What role does "meaning" play in their lives? Ask them about their core values and the role they play in their success.

- Watch and discuss with others provocative films that probe the role of values and questions of morality and ethics (for example, *Doubt* (2002), called the "first moral thriller"). Start a movie club for this purpose. Make a list of such films and circulate it.

- Do an ethics "styles" assessment of your family members. Your company. Your church. Etc. How might the knowledge you gain affect relationships or be put to use in problem solving?

• Identify three Big Moments in your life and do a "drilling analysis" of each one of them to discover what core values emerge. In terms of the Three Essentials, where do they seem to cluster (doing right, being true, seeking good)? Discuss the impact they've had on your life. How might they be expressed more fully in your current life?

• Try to find out which companies in your area engage in "purpose marketing." Interview their managers and employees (on a casual basis or through invitations to speak to your group or organization). What are their core values (i.e., those of their company)? How effective are they as the basis for doing business? What difference do they seem to be making in your community? What impact do they have on the company's employees?

SOURCES & WORKS CITED

Autry, James. *Love and Profit: The Art of Caring Leadership* (William Morrow, 1992).

Collins, Jim. *Built to Last* (HarperBusiness, 2004).

Covey, Stephen. *Seven Habits of Highly Effective People* (Free Press, 2004, Revised Edition).

Driscoll, Dawn-Marie and Hoffman, W. Michael. *Ethics Matters: How to Implement Values-Driven Management* (Bentley Center for Business Ethics, 2000).

Frankl, Victor. *Man's Search for Meaning* (Beacon Press, 2006).

Greenleaf, Robert. *Servant Leadership: A Journey into the Nature of Legitimate Power and Greatness* (Paulist Press, 2012).

Hargrove, Robert. *Masterful Coaching* (Pfeiffer, 2008).

Kidder, Rushworth. *How Good People Make Tough Choices: Resolving the Dilemmas of Ethical Living* (Harper, 2009 Edition).

—*The Ethics Recession: Reflections on the Moral Underpinnings of the Current Economic Crisis* (Institute for Global Ethics, 2009).

Singer, Peter. *How Are We to Live?: Ethics in an Age of Self-Interest* (Prometheus Books, 1995).

Warren, Rick. *The Purpose Driven Life: What on Earth Am I Here For?* (Zondervan, 2012, Special Anniversary Edition).

OPPORTUNITIES

Opportunities are available to work with the author on an individual and organizational basis to apply the insights and methods found in this book.

THE ETHICS COACH®
www.ethicscoach.net

Consultation, Coaching & Training
• *Custom Individual & Executive Coaching*
• *Ethics Training & Integrity Culture Building*
(business consultation and training)
• *1-3 Day Training & Retreat Experiences*
(customized leadership events for business managers, educators and religious leaders)

Online Coaching Packages
• *Individual Solutions*

• *Business & Entrepreneur Solutions*
• *Academic Solutions*

"Ethics Unplugged" Blog
www.ethicsunplugged.com
An interactive exploration of contemporary issues viewed though the ethical vision outlined in this book.

ABOUT THE AUTHOR

STEPHEN SWECKER is a college teacher of ethics, religion and social problems; an award-winning magazine editor and columnist; and editor of and contributor to numerous books, including *Hard Ball on Holy Ground* (BW Press, 2005), *Wells of Wisdom* (Pilgrim Press, 2005) and *Faith and the Common Good* (Rider Green, 2014). Steve graduated from Boston University Graduate School, Wesley Theological Seminary and West Virginia University. He is a certified life coach and member of the International Regulator of Coaching and Mentoring CIC. He and his wife Kathy live in Maine.

.